SIMPLE STEPS TO SENTE

A HANDBOOK FOR LEARNING ENGLISH GRAMMAR AND USAGE

Charlene Tess

ABOUT THE AUTHOR

Charlene Tess taught English and creative writing to high school students and adults for over thirty-five years. She is listed in Who's Who in America. She is the author of the series of *Simple Steps to Sentence Sense* grammar workbooks and writes educational resources for teacherspayteachers.com.

Her novels are available as Kindle eBooks on Amazon.com. She co-writes romantic suspense novels with her sister Judi Thompson under the pen name Tess Thompson.

CONTACT INFORMATION

Amazon Book Page: www.amazon.com/author/charlenetess
Email: booksbycharlenetess@gmail.com
Website: www.booksbycharlenetess.com
Like my Facebook Fan Page: http://www.facebook.com/booksbycharlenetess
Subscribe to my newsletter to receive grammar tips and free educational products.
http://eepurl.com/flKrg

FORWARD

I have been teaching grammar and writing since 1964. I suppose that fact is sufficient to qualify me as a senior citizen, but I hope it will also qualify me as an experienced teacher who might have something to tell you that would be helpful whether you are a teacher, a student, or a writer. Truthfully, anyone can benefit from following the simple steps in this book. I have used them to teach thousands of young people and adults to analyze English sentences and then write their own.

This book is different from the three other *Simple Steps to Sentence Sense* editions. (*Simple Steps to Sentence Sense for High School* was first published in 1996, *Simple Steps to Sentence Sense for Middle School* in 2010, and *Simple Steps to Sentence Sense for Elementary Students and ESL Students* in 2011). The difference is that this book contains instructional material and tells you how to analyze and write sentences correctly, but it is not intended to be a workbook. Instead, it is a handbook to use as a reference as you teach or learn English grammar.
I did include a link to a set of printable practice exercises that you can use while working with this book. You can access them online at this link: https://bit.ly/SStoSAExercises.

Please note, that after you finish the steps in this book, you will know how to analyze sentences, and you will know how to write sentences correctly. Whether or not you wish to practice what you have learned is entirely up to you.

If you are planning to use my method of sentence analysis to teach your students, you will save yourself hours of preparation if you purchase one of my *Simple Steps to Sentence Sense* workbooks that contain notes, document projection pages, group practice exercises, individual practice exercises, tests, writing connection pages, and the answers.

The three *Simple Steps to Sentence Sense* workbooks are only a click away. You will find them on my Amazon page. www.amazon.com/author/charlenetess.

So, let's get started on the 8 Simple Steps to Sentence Analysis!

HOW DOES MY GRAMMAR PROGRAM WORK?

As a very young teacher, I realized that in order for students to learn, they need to follow certain steps. Just as children usually learn to crawl, then pull themselves up into a standing position, and then take their first steps, so do students of a language need to learn to recognize the parts of a sentence and use them correctly before they can become effective writers of paragraphs and longer works.

Those who are learning to write well need to examine and understand the structure of a sentence in the same way that a seamstress and homebuilder need a pattern and a blueprint. Once students have mastered the structure of an English sentence, they can move on to writing dynamic paragraphs and compositions.

It's all about the sequence in which we learn to analyze sentences. Traditional English grammar textbooks and even some modern ones are confusing and difficult to use because they do not present the material in the proper sequence.

The steps I present in this book are logical and effective. I know that they work because I began presenting my lessons in this order in 1964. These steps have been tested on thousands of students and adults. If you follow the steps in order and do not skip any of them, you will be amazed at how easy it is to analyze a sentence and then write sentences of your own based on the same pattern.

These are the 8 steps in the order you should learn them:

1. Find the prepositional phrase(s).
2. Find the verb and its helping verbs. Determine if the main verb is an action verb or a linking verb.
3. Find the subject.
4. Look for complements (direct object, indirect object, objective complement, predicate nominative, and predicate adjective)
5. Find the adjectives and adverbs.
6. Find the phrases. (appositive, adjective, adverb, and noun)
7. Find the clauses. (independent, adjective, adverb, and noun)
8. Classify the Sentences. (simple, compound, complex, or compound/complex).

STEP 1 - Find and eliminate the prepositional phrase.

Put [brackets]around the prepositional phrases.

A prepositional phrase is a group of words that begins with a preposition and ends with a noun or pronoun. (The prepositions in the following examples are in bold.)

Example: The birds sat **under** the trees and searched **for** food.

Prepositional Phrases: "under the trees" and "for food"

The noun or pronoun that ends this type of phrase is called the "object of the preposition."

Example: "under the trees" and "for food"

Object of the Preposition: "trees" and "food"

The main parts of a sentence (like a subject and verb) are NEVER inside a prepositional phrase, so it helps to find all the prepositional phrases first and eliminate them from the sentence before analyzing it. To remove the prepositional phrases from a sentence so you can find the subject and verb easily, simply place [brackets] around the phrase, beginning with the preposition and ending with the object of the preposition.

To find the beginning of a prepositional phrase, look for a preposition.

Common Prepositions

aboard	below	for	past
about	beneath	from	since
above	beside	in	through
across	besides	inside	throughout
after	between	into	to
against	beyond	like	toward
along	but	near	under
amid	except	of	underneath
among	by	off	until
around	concerning	on	unto
as	despite	onto	up
at	down	out	upon
before	during	outside	with
behind	except	over	within
			without

Compound Prepositions

according to	by way of	in spite of
ahead of	in addition to	instead of
aside from	in case of	on account of
because of	in front of	out of
by means of	in place of	prior to
	in regard to	

To find the object of the preposition, look for a noun or pronoun that answers the question **whom? or what?** The first word in a prepositional phrase is the preposition, and the last word is the object of the preposition. The words in between are adjectives and adverbs.

Example: One of the girls in the new blue car is my sister.
One [**of** the girls] [**in** the new blue car] is my sister.
"Of" and "in" are prepositions. "Girls" and "car" are objects of the preposition, and the words "the", "new", and "blue" are adjectives.

Sometimes prepositions are compound, which means more than one of them has been used in a single phrase.
Example: [**In case of** fire**]**, use the nearest exit.
"In case of" is a **compound preposition**
"fire" is the object of the compound preposition

Sometimes even the object of the preposition is compound.
If so, the objects are joined by a conjunction (and, but, or, etc.).

Example: Barbara was walking [**with** John **and** me].
The word "and" is a conjunction, so...
"John" & "me" are both objects of the preposition.

Note: A comma usually follows an introductory prepositional phrase (one that begins the sentence).

Example Sentence A
Under the trees, lay an old yellow dog.
Find the preposition (under). Ask what? or whom? to find the object of the preposition (trees). Put the prepositional phrase in brackets. This shortens the sentence and makes it easier to find the remaining sentence elements. Note the comma because this was an introductory prepositional phrase.
[**Under** the **trees**], lay an old yellow dog.

Example Sentence B
I was driving my car within the speed limit.
Find the preposition; find the object of the preposition; enclose the prepositional phrase in brackets. I was driving my car [**within** the speed **limit**].

STEP 2 - Find the verb.

Place <u>two lines</u> under the verb phrases.
The verb is the most important part of the sentence. It is a word that expresses mental or physical action (like "think" or "run"), or it expresses a state-of-being (like "am" or "became").

If a word is a verb, it has an "ing" form.
Example: run = running, took = taking
The "ing" form of all forms of the verb "to be" = being
Verbs can be classified as **ACTION** or **LINKING** verbs.

Linking Verbs
is   am   are   was   were   be   been   being

Verbs that can be Action or Linking depending upon the sentence in which they appear.
*appear *become *became *feel *grow * look* remain * seem * smell * sound *stay * taste *turn

Use the *Substitution Test* below to determine if the verb is action or linking.
SUBSTITUTION TEST: If you can replace the verb with a form of the verb "to be" (is, am, are, was, were, be, been or being), the verb in the sentence is a linking verb. If you cannot replace it, the verb in the sentence is an action verb.

Example:
A. The cake tasted good.
B. The cook tasted the cake.
In sentence A, "tasted" can be replaced with the linking verb "was." In this sentence, "tasted" is a linking verb.
In sentence B, "tasted" cannot be replaced with a linking verb. In this sentence, "tasted" is an action verb.

HINT: Do not test all verbs. Only test the verbs with an * above.

A verb phrase consists of the main verb and any helping verbs that go with it.

Common Helping Verbs
is am are was were be been being do does did has have had
can may will shall could would should might must

The maximum number of words in a verb phrase is four. The main verb, not the helping verbs, will determine if the verb is an action verb or a linking verb.
Example: will have been singing = verb phrase
"Will" "have" and "been" are helping verbs. The main verb, "singing" is an action verb.
Be aware that adverbs frequently interrupt verb phrases.

Common Adverbs That Frequently Interrupt Verb Phrases
*sometimes * never * not * always * usually * often * certainly * evidently * hardly
* scarcely * seldom * frequently

Example: have **certainly** been given
"Certainly" is not a verb; it is an adverb. It "interrupts" or comes between the helping verbs and the main verb in the verb phrase.

Sometimes the verb is compound. Compound verbs are joined by conjunctions. (and, but, or).
Example: She ate candy **and** drank a coke.

In an interrogative sentence (a sentence that asks a question), the normal word order is inverted or changed around. To make it easier to find the verb phrase, mentally change it into a statement before you analyze it.
Example: Will he be going with us? = He will be going [with us.]

EXAMPLE A
USING STEPS 1 AND 2
He could have given me better directions to the party.
Step 1 Find the prepositional phrase(s) and enclose in [brackets].
He could have given me better directions [to the party].
Step 2 Find the verb phrase and underline it twice. Determine if the main verb is Action or Linking.
He could have given me better directions [to the party]
"could" and "have" are helping verbs
"given" is an action verb

EXAMPLE B
USING STEPS 1 AND 2
My father did not give me a chance.
Step 1 Find the prepositional phrase(s) and enclose in [brackets].
[none]
Step 2 Find the verb phrase and underline it twice. Determine if the main verb is Action or Linking.
My father did not give me a chance.
"did" is a helping verb
"not" is an adverb that interrupts the verb phrase
"give" is an action verb

STEP 3 - Find the subject.

The subject of a sentence is what the sentence is about. It will be a noun or pronoun that usually appears in front of the verb and tells "who" or "what" performed the action of the verb or is linked to other information in the sentence by the verb. Draw one line under the <u>subject.</u>
To find the simple subject, LOOK IN FRONT OF THE VERB and ask "WHO?" or "WHAT?"

Example Sentence: "John is late." Ask: Who is late?
John answers that question, so <u>*John*</u> is the subject of the sentence.

Sentence: "He is tall." Ask: Who is tall?
He answers that question, so <u>*He*</u> is the subject of the sentence.

Sometimes the subject will be compound. If so, it will be joined by a conjunction (and, but, or).
Example: <u>Maria</u> and <u>Omar</u> will lead the parade.

Maria answers the question "Who?" about the verb, but Omar answers the question, as well. Therefore, they are BOTH the subject of the sentence. The conjunction "and" between them tells you the subject is compound (made up of more than one).

Although the subject is usually found in front of the verb, there are four times that the subject will be found in a different position in the sentence.

THE SUBJECT WILL NOT BE IN FRONT OF THE VERB WHEN AND IF:
1) The sentence begins with a prepositional phrase.
Example: [Under the bridge] lay the <u>cow</u>.
Remember: The subject will NEVER be found inside a prepositional phrase.

2) The sentence begins with the words "here" or "there."
Example: "Here is my <u>friend</u>." "There is my <u>car</u>."
Note: The words "here and "there" are adverbs and are NEVER the subject of the sentence.

3) The sentence asks a question (an interrogative sentence).
Example: "Is <u>he</u> the manager of the motel?"
Hint: Put the words back in order, and it's easy to find the subject.
<u>He</u> is the manager of the motel.

4) The sentence is a command or polite request (an imperative sentence).
The subject of an imperative sentence is an understood "you."
Example: "Pass the salt." - MEANS - (<u>You</u>) pass the salt.
(The subject of this sentence is implied, not stated. The subject is "understood" to be in front of the verb, but it is NOT written there.)

Example A
Using Steps 1-3
There is no need for your anger.
Step 1 Find the prepositional phrase(s).
There is no need [for your anger].
Step 2 Find the verb phrase and determine if the verb is an action or a linking verb.
There <u>is</u> no need [for your anger].
("Is" is a linking verb.)
Step 3 Find the subject.
There <u>is</u> no <u>need</u> [for your anger]. "<u>Need</u>" is the subject.
(Remember, the words "here" and "there" will never be the subject of the sentence.)

Example B
Using Steps 1-3
Stand here and hold my place in the line.
Step 1
[in the line]
Step 2
<u>stand</u> , <u>hold</u> (Compound verbs are joined by the conjunction "and.")
Step 3
<u>You</u> (This sentence is a command. The subject is implied, not stated.)

STEP 4 - Find the complements.

Words that complete the thoughts of a sentence are called **COMPLEMENTS.** There are two kinds of complements: those that **FOLLOW ACTION VERBS** and those that **FOLLOW LINKING VERBS.**

Complements that follow an **ACTION VERB** include: a **DIRECT OBJECT**, an **INDIRECT OBJECT**, and an **OBJECTIVE COMPLEMENT**.

Complements that follow a **LINKING VERB** include:
PREDICATE NOMINATIVES and **PREDICATE ADJECTIVES**

Follow these steps to find complements:
1. **If a sentence has an action verb, look for a DIRECT OBJECT. A direct object (D.O.)** is a noun or pronoun that completes the meaning of the sentence. **To find the direct object:** Say the subject, say the verb, and then ask whom? or what? The answer will be the direct object:
Example: Ted hit **Sam**. Ted hit whom?
"Sam" is the direct object.

Sometimes the direct object is compound, with a conjunction between two or more items:
Example: I like **cake** and ice **cream**. I like what?
BOTH **"cake"** and **"cream"** are direct objects here.

2. **If a sentence has a direct object, look for an INDIRECT OBJECT or an OBJECTIVE COMPLEMENT.**
      a) An **indirect object (I.o.)** is a noun or pronoun that precedes the direct object and answers the questions "to whom?" or "for whom?" The words of the sentence would come in this order: Subject, Verb, **Indirect Object**, Direct Object. (The indirect object would precede the direct object.)

NOTE: A Sentence CANNOT Have An INDIRECT OBJECT Unless There Is A DIRECT OBJECT.

To find the indirect object: Say the subject, say the verb, say the direct object, and then ask "to whom?" or "for whom?"
Example: The book club sent its members cards.

Club (the subject) sent (verb) cards (direct object) to whom?
"Members" is the answer, and thus it is the indirect object.

Indirect Objects can be compound, meaning there will be a conjunction (and, but, or) between two indirect objects.
Example: I gave **Maria** and **Pablo** a ride to church.
Ask yourself: I gave a ride "to whom?" Both **"Maria"** and **"Pablo"** were given a ride to church, so **BOTH** are indirect objects in this sentence.

b) An **objective complement (O.C.)** is a word that **follows a direct object and renames or describes it.**
It may be a **noun or an adjective**. The word order would be: subject, verb, direct object, objective complement.

Example of RENAMING the direct object: We consider her a good player.
"Player" follows the direct object "her" and **renames** it, so **"player"** is an objective complement.

Example of DESCRIBING the direct object: Many call him **unbeatable**.
"Unbeatable" follows the direct object "him" and describes it, so **"unbeatable"** is an objective complement.
Sometimes the objective complement is compound.
Example: Some think him **arrogant** and **rude**.
BOTH "arrogant" and "rude" follow the direct object and describe it,
so BOTH are objective complements.

An objective complement frequently occurs in sentences with these verbs: "appoint," "call," "choose," "consider," "elect," "find," "make," "keep," "name," and "think."

3. If the verb is **LINKING,** look for a **predicate nominative** or a **predicate adjective.**

a) A **predicate nominative** (PN.) is a noun or pronoun that **renames the subject**.
Example: He is my **friend**. "Friend" renames the subject "he."
"Friend" is a **predicate nominative**.
The pronouns which can be predicate nominatives are: "I," "we," "you," "she," "he," "it," and "they.")
Example: It was she. "She" renames the subject

b) A **predicate adjective (P.A.)** is an adjective that follows a linking verb and **modifies the subject** of the sentence.
Example: That man is really **handsome**. "Handsome" modifies the subject "man."
"Handsome" is a predicate adjective.

c) **Predicate adjectives AND predicate nominatives** may be compound.
Example: I am happy and sad.
BOTH "happy" and "sad" are predicate adjectives in this sentence.

A SIMPLE TEST TO SEE IF A WORD IS A PREDICATE NOMINATIVE (P.N.) OR A PREDICATE ADJECTIVE (P.A.) IS TO TRY TO MAKE THE WORD PLURAL.

Predicate Adjectives CANNOT be made plural.
Example: She is **pretty**.
In this sentence, "pretty" is a **predicate adjective** because you CANNOT make the word "pretty" plural. ("prettys"?)

Predicate Nominatives CAN be made plural.
Examples: She is a **girl**. It was he.
In these sentences, "girl" is a **predicate nominative** because you CAN make the word "girl" plural - (girls) and "he" is a predicate nominative because the plural of "he" is "they."

REVIEW of COMPLEMENTS

If there is a word following the verb that completes the meaning of the sentence, it is called a complement.

An **action verb** can have three types of complements: direct object, indirect object, and objective complement.

A **linking verb** can have two types of complements: predicate nominative or predicate adjective.

Since the verb determines the type of complement, you must determine if the verb is action or linking before you look for the complement.

Example A (Using Steps 1-4)
Maxine should not have given me a hard time about my new hairstyle.
Step 1 Find the prepositional phrase.
[about my new hairstyle]
Step 2 Find the verb phrase. Determine if the main verb is an action or a linking verb.
should have given ("should" and "have" are helping verbs; "not" is an adverb, "given" is an action verb)
Step 3 Find the subject.
Maxine
Step 4 Find the complement(s)
Since the verb is action, look for a direct object.
Maxine should have given what? **time** "Time" is a direct object.
Because you found a direct object, look for an indirect object or an objective complement.
Maxine should have given time to whom? **me** "Me" is an indirect object.
* Maxine should not have given **me** a hard **time** [about my new hairstyle].

Example B (Using Steps 1-4)
The doctor believes a cure for her illness impossible.
Step 1
[for her illness]
Step 2
believes (action verb)
Step 3
doctor (subject)
Step 4
Since the verb is action, look for a direct object.
The doctor believes a cure for her illness impossible. "Cure" is a direct object.
Because you found a direct object, look for an indirect object or an objective complement.
The doctor believes a cure for her illness impossible.
("Impossible" describes the direct object. "**Impossible**" is an objective complement.
* The doctor believes a cure [for her illness] impossible.

Example C (Using Steps 1-4)

The dancers seemed tired after the performance.
Step 1 [after the performance]
Step 2 <u>seemed</u> "Seem" is on the list of verbs that can be either action or linking. If you use the substitution test, you will find that in this sentence, "seemed" is a linking verb.
Step 3 <u>dancers</u>
Step 4 Tired is a predicate adjective that describes the subject.
* The <u>dancers</u> <u>seemed</u> **tired** [after the performance]

STEP 5 - Adjectives and Adverbs

AN ADJECTIVE MODIFIES A NOUN OR A PRONOUN. (Modifies means that it describes the word to make its meaning more definite.) They answer the questions, "Which one?" "What kind?" or "How many?"

Examples: What kind of car?   **race** car
                      Which one?   **this** car
                      How many cars?   **several** cars

You have already studied the predicate adjective and the objective complement adjective, but there are other kinds of adjectives, as well.

A) The **articles** are the most frequently used adjectives: **"a"**, **"an"**, and **"the."**

B) Whenever you use a possessive pronoun in a sentence, consider it an adjective: "**my**" pencil, "**your**" problem, "**his**" father, "**her**" keys, "**its**" collar, "**our**" house, "**their**" mail, "**someone's**" job, "**everyone's**" responsibility, etc.

C) **Other pronouns** can also be used as adjectives: "**this**" book, "**that**" hat, "**these**" shoes, "**those**" coats, etc.

D) Sometimes you will find nouns used as adjectives: "**potato**" salad, or "**dog**" food, etc.

E) **Possessive nouns** are also used as adjectives: "**Karen's**" coat, or "**king's**" crown, etc.

F) Sometimes **verbs** are used as adjectives. If so, they are PARTICIPLES or INFINITIVES.

Examples: **dancing** bear   The one **to buy** is the green one.
             (**dancin**g is a participle) (**to buy** is an infinitive)

ADVERBS

AN ADVERB IS A WORD THAT MODIFIES A VERB, AN ADJECTIVE, OR ANOTHER
ADVERB IN A SENTENCE.

Adverbs answer the questions, "Where?", "When?", "How?", "To what extent?", or "Under what condition?"

A) Adverbs can **modify the verb**: "I moved **forward**." (where?); "I **gladly** moved." (how?); "I moved **immediately**." (when?); "She **scarcely** moved." (to what extent?)

B) Adverbs **can modify an adjective**: "Mike is an **especially** good swimmer." (tells "to what extent the swimming is good")

C) An adverb **can also modify another adverb**: "Max is almost always late." (tells "to what extent")

D) Adverbs can be found next to the words they modify, or they **can introduce questions and clauses**: "When will you finish the dishes?" (introduces a question); "**When** you finish the dishes, we can go shopping." (introduces a clause)

E) **Sometimes nouns are used as adverbs**: "I am going **home**." (tells "**where**" I am going)

NOTE: Many adverbs end in "ly." However, there are many words that end in "ly" that are not adverbs. In fact, several adjectives also end in "ly" such as "early, only, friendly, daily, etc." When you are identifying a word, do not depend upon its ending to help you determine its part of speech. Instead, use the questions that adjectives and adverbs answer to tell you what role the word plays in that sentence.

Important: After you have completed Step 4, the words that remain in the sentence that have not been identified will be modifiers (and the conjunctions that join them if they are compound).

Example A
Using Steps 1-5

We looked around the corner slowly and warily.
Step 1 [around the corner]
Step 2 <u>looked</u> = action verb
Step 3 <u>We</u> = subject
Step 4 There are no complements in this sentence.
Step 5 Note the words that have not been identified in this sentence:
~~We looked around the corner~~ **slowly and warily**. All the other words have been identified.
Slowly answers the question "how?" *Slowly* is an adverb modifying *looked*.
Warily answers the question "how?" *Warily* is an adverb modifying *looked*.
And is a conjunction that joins the two adverbs.

Example B
Using Steps 1-5

Three happy cheerleaders jumped excitedly on the sidelines of the field.
Step 1 [on the sidelines] [of the field]
Step 2 <u>jumped</u> = action verb
Step 3 <u>cheerleaders</u> = subject
Step 4 There are no complements in this sentence.

Note the words that have not been identified in this sentence.
Three happy ~~cheerleaders jumped~~ **excitedly** ~~on the sidelines of the field~~.
Step 5 *Three* and *happy (answer the question which one?)* are adjectives that modify *cheerleaders*.
　　　And is a conjunction that joins the two adjectives.
Step 6 *Excitedly* is an adverb (answers the question *how?*) that modifies *jumped*.

Example C Using Steps 1-5

The cook gave each lucky person in the restaurant a sample of his signature dish.

Step 1 [in the restaurant] [of his signature dish]

Step 2 <u>gave</u> is an action verb

Step 3 <u>cook</u> is the subject

Step 4 **sample** is the direct object (answers the question "what"?)

   person is the indirect object (answers the question "to whom"?)

The ~~cook gave~~ **each lucky** ~~person in the restaurant~~ **a** ~~sample of his signature dish.~~

Step 5 *the, each, lucky,* and *a* are adjectives

Step 6 – Phrases

Besides the prepositional phrase, a sentence may contain **VERBAL PHRASES** which are formed from verbs but are used as other parts of speech. **The three verbals are: participles, gerunds, and infinitives.**

PARTICIPLE AND PARTICIPIAL PHRASE.

A participle is a verb that is used as an adjective. It usually ends in "ing," "en," "ed," or "d." A participial phrase may contain a participle, modifiers, prepositional phrases or an object of the participle. If a participle is preceded by a helping verb, it is considered a verb.

Examples: A)   The **developing** storm looks dangerous.

B)   The storm, **developing rapidly**, looks dangerous. (This participial phrase is made up of the participle **developing** and the adverb **rapidly,** which modifies storm.)

C)   The boy **waving the flag** is my cousin. (Since a participle is a verb, it can have an object. **Waving** is a participle and **flag** is the object of the participle.)
D)   The boy **was waving** the flag. (**was waving** is the verb phrase)

NOTE: The participle and participial phrase should be placed as close as possible to the noun or pronoun it modifies. In examples A and B, the participle *developing* modifies *storm*. In example C, the participle *waving* modifies *boy*.

GERUND AND GERUND PHRASE

A gerund is a verb that is used as a noun. It always ends in "ing." It will function in the sentence just as a noun does and may be used as the subject, direct object, indirect object, predicate nominative, or the object of the preposition. A gerund phrase may contain a gerund, modifiers, prepositional phrases or an object of the gerund.

Examples: A) **Skating** is my hobby. (Skating is a gerund used as the subject.)
B)   She enjoys **singing in the choir**. (*Singing* is a gerund used as the direct object, *in the choir* is a prepositional phrase.)
C)   His favorite exercise is **walking briskly in the park at noon**. (*Walking* is a gerund used as a predicate nominative; *briskly* is an adverb that modifies the gerund *walking*; *in the park* and *at noon* are prepositional phrases.)
D)   He won the game by **kicking a field goal**. (*Kicking* is a gerund used as the object of the preposition "by"; *a* and *field* are adjectives that modify the object of the gerund *goal*.

HINT: To determine the function of a gerund phrase, first see if there is a preposition in front of it. If so, the gerund phrase will function as the object of the preposition. If there is none, look at the position of the phrase in the sentence. If the phrase is at the beginning of the sentence, it is the subject. If it's at the end of the sentence, it will be a direct object or a predicate nominative depending on the verb in the sentence.

Note the position of the gerund:
preposition <**gerund**> = object of the preposition
<**gerund**> verb = subject
action verb <**gerund**> = direct object
linking verb <**gerund**> = predicate nominative

NOTE: To distinguish between a participle ending in "ing" and a gerund, try removing the *ing* word from the sentence and see if a complete thought remains. A gerund cannot be removed; a participle can.

Example A

Eating popcorn is one of the best things about going to the movies.
< Eating popcorn > The gerund phrase is at the beginning of the sentence. It is used as a subject.
I love eating popcorn at the movies.
< Eating popcorn > The gerund phrase is at the end of the sentence and follows an action verb. It is used as a direct object.

The problem with eating popcorn is that it is addictive.
< eating popcorn > The gerund phrase has a preposition in front of it. It is used as an object of the preposition.

My weakness is eating popcorn.
< eating popcorn > The gerund phrase is at the end of the sentence and follows a linking verb. It is used as a predicate nominative.

INFINITIVE AND INFINITIVE PHRASE

An infinitive is a verb that is generally used as a noun, but can also be used as an adjective or adverb. It is usually introduced by the word "to." It will function in the sentence as an adjective, adverb, or noun.

> **Examples:** A) **To win** is his ambition. **(infinitive as subject)**
> B) He lacked the will **to live. (infinitive as adjective)**
> C) We read **to learn. (infinitive as adverb)**

Sometimes the word "to" is understood (implied).

> **Example:** "Help me **mow** the lawn." - **means** - "Help me **to mow** the lawn."

An infinitive phrase may contain an infinitive, modifiers, prepositional phrases, or an object of the infinitive.

> **Example:** I know there is a way **to solve this problem.** (This is an infinitive phrase used as an adjective modifying *way*: **to solve** is the infinitive; **this** is an adjective; **problem** is the object of the infinitive)

NOTE: DO NOT CONFUSE THE INFINITIVE WITH A PREPOSITIONAL PHRASE BEGINNING WITH "TO." AN INFINITIVE IS FOLLOWED BY A VERB; A PREPOSITION 1S FOLLOWED BY A NOUN OR PRONOUN.

> Examples: A) I wanted <to sing> = infinitive
> B) I went [to church] = prepositional phrase

Besides a prepositional phrase and the three kinds of verbal phrases above, sentences may also contain an APPOSITIVE PHRASE.

THE APPOSITIVE AND APPOSITIVE PHRASE

An appositive is a noun that re-names, explains, or identifies another noun.

Example: Mr. Smith, my teacher, is kind.
(The appositive, **teacher**, RE-NAMES the noun **Mr. Smith**.)

An appositive phrase consists of the appositive and its modifiers. It usually follows the word it explains or identifies, but it may precede it.

Examples of Phrases

Example A

The flu, a serious threat to the elderly and the young, can be prevented with a shot.

Phrase: a serious threat to the elderly and the young

Type of phrase: appositive phrase

Function of phrase: renames "flu."

Objects in phrase: ~~none~~

Prepositional phrases found within phrase: [to the elderly and the young]

Modifiers found inside the phrase: a, serious = adjectives

Example B

Running marathons once a year is her goal for life.

Phrase: running marathons once a year

Type of phrase: gerund

Function of phrase: subject

Objects in phrase: marathons

Prepositional phrases found within phrase: [once a year]

Modifiers found inside the phrase: none

Example C

Covered with catsup, the fries were delicious.

Phrase: covered with catsup

Type of phrase: participial phrase

Function of phrase: adjective modifying "fries"

Objects in phrase: none

Prepositional phrases found within phrase: [with catsup]

Modifiers found inside the phrase: none

Step 7 – Clauses

You will need to refer to these lists when working with clauses:

Relative Pronouns

(Introduce Adjective and Noun Clauses)

who
whose
whom
which
what
that
whoever
whomever
whichever
whatever
when and where (adverbs that sometimes introduce adjective clauses)

Subordinating Conjunctions

(Introduce Adverb Clauses)

after	so that
although	than
as	though
as if	that
as much as	till
because	unless
before	until
now	when
if	whenever
in order that	whether
in as much as	where
provided	wherever
since	while

Questions Adjectives answer:
which one?
what kind?
how many?

Questions Adverbs answer:
when?
where?
why?
how?
to what extent?
under what condition?

Conjunctions
(connect words, phrases, or clauses)
and, but, or, for, nor, yet
either...or
neither...nor
both...and
not (only)...but (also)
whether...or

Conjunctive Adverbs
(connect main clauses)
accordingly, again, also, as a result, besides, **consequently**, finally, for example, further, furthermore, hence, **however**, in addition, indeed, in fact, in particular, instead, likewise, meanwhile, **moreover**, namely

nevertheless, otherwise, still, that is, then, **therefore**, **thus**

INDEPENDENT AND SUBORDINATE CLAUSES

A **clause** is a group of words that contains a subject and a verb. There are two main types of clauses:

The **independent clause** is one that makes sense standing alone (a simple sentence).
Example: "Today is Wednesday."

The **subordinate clause** (also called a **dependent clause**) is one that does not make complete sense if standing alone. A subordinate clause may be used in. three ways in a sentence: as an adjective, as an adverb, or as a noun. (The example below is used as an adverb.)

Example: "Because today is Wednesday"
The clause (because today is Wednesday) does not make sense alone. It is "dependent" on other words in the sentence to make sense.

The **combination of independent and subordinate clauses** creates interesting sentences.
Examples: A. (Because today is Wednesday), **I set out the trash**.
        B. **It must be Wednesday** (because I set out the trash).
Note: The subordinate clause in each sentence above has been identified by parentheses. The independent clause is in bold type.

ADJECTIVE, ADVERB, AND NOUN CLAUSES

THE ADJECTIVE CLAUSE is a subordinate clause used as an adjective to modify a noun or pronoun. It begins with a relative pronoun or with the adverbs, "when" and "where." In some instances, the word which connects the clause is omitted:

    Examples:
    A. He read the book **that I gave him**. (adjective clause, modifying *book*, introduced by the relative pronoun *that*)

    B. He read the book **I gave him**. (adjective clause, modifying *book*, omitting the introductory relative pronoun *that*)

An adjective clause usually modifies the noun or pronoun that immediately precedes it. Therefore, an adjective clause will never be found at the beginning of the sentence. An adjective clause will contain a subject and verb and any other element that can be found in a sentence. Often, the relative pronoun is one of the important elements in the clause.

    Example: The man **to whom I am referring** is the president of the organization.

In this clause, **whom** is the object of the preposition **to**. The subject of the clause is **I**, and the verb is **am referring**.

THE ADVERB CLAUSE is used as an adverb and usually modifies the verb in the independent clause. It begins with a subordinating conjunction or with an adverb (refer to page 16). Unless it is very short, an adverb clause that appears at the beginning of the sentence should be followed by a comma.

Example: Because the water was cold, we did not swim.

The subordinating conjunction **because** introduces the adverb clause which modifies the verb **did swim** in the independent clause.

An adverb clause will contain a subject and verb and any other element that can be found in a sentence.
Example: After we had bathed in the stream, we felt refreshed.

In this clause, **we** is the subject, **had bathed** is the verb, and **in the stream** is a prepositional phrase: The clause is introduced by the subordinating conjunction **after**. This clause modifies the verb **felt** in the independent clause.

THE NOUN CLAUSE is used as a noun and can be the subject, direct object, predicate nominative, or object of the preposition in the sentence. It usually begins with a relative pronoun (refer to page 16).

Examples:
"**What you think** is important to me." = noun clause used as subject
"Do you know **what the answer to the question is?** = noun clause used as direct object
"The truth is **what I want to hear from you.** = noun clause used as predicate nominative
"Give the money to **whomever you wish.**" = noun clause used as the object of the preposition

A noun clause may contain a subject and verb and any other element that can be found in a sentence.
Example: I know that he loves me.

The noun clause is used as the direct object; **that** is a relative pronoun; **he** is the subject of the clause; **loves** is the verb; and **me** is the direct object in the adjective clause.

HINT: To determine the function of a noun clause, first see if there is a preposition in front of it. If so, the noun clause will function as the object of the preposition. If there isn't a preposition, look at the position of the clause in the sentence. If the clause is at the beginning of the sentence, it is the subject. If it is at the end of the sentence, it will be a direct object or a predicate nominative (depending on the verb in the independent clause).

Note the patterns below:

preposition (**noun clause**) = noun clause functions as the object of the preposition
(**noun clause**) verb = noun clause functions as the subject
action verb (**noun clause**) = noun clause functions as the direct object
linking verb (**noun clause**) = noun clause functions as a predicate nominative

NOTE: HERE ARE SOME TRICKS TO DISTINGUISH BETWEEN THE THREE TYPES OF CLAUSES:

- First, always try removing the clause from the sentence (a noun clause cannot be removed)
- If the clause can be removed, use the questions that adjectives and adverbs answer to determine the type of   clause.
- Remember that adjective clauses cannot be at the beginning of the sentence.
- Sometimes the introductory word will help since adjective clauses usually begin with relative pronouns and adverb clauses usually begin with subordinating conjunctions.(This method is the least reliable. For example, the word "that" can introduce all three types of clauses.)
- Remember that an introductory adverb clause is usually followed by a comma.

Step 8 – Classifying Sentences

There are four types of sentences: simple, compound, complex, and compound-complex:

1) The SIMPLE sentence contains ONE INDEPENDENT clause.

Example: The man standing in the doorway is my Uncle Fred.

Notice that the sentence does not have to be short to be simple. It can have many phrases and still be a "simple" sentence. In fact, parts of a simple sentence may be compound, as in the example below:
> Example: Mary and Tom are going to the dance together. (This sentence contains a
> compound subject.)

2) The COMPOUND sentence contains TWO INDEPENDENT clauses joined by a conjunction, such as "and" "but," "or," "nor," "yet," or "for". In such sentences, the conjunction should be preceded by a comma.

If the independent clauses are very short and closely related, they may be joined by a semicolon (;).

Examples: A) Marty is the leader of the group, **but** he is not the best person for the job.
B) I like dogs; he likes cats.

NOTE: Sometimes the independent clauses are joined by conjunctive adverbs such as: *moreover, nevertheless, therefore, however, or consequently*. If so, the conjunctive adverb is preceded by a semicolon and followed by a comma.

Example: He is an expert in this field; **therefore**, the company hired him.

3) The COMPLEX sentence contains at least ONE INDEPENDENT clause & ONE DEPENDENT clause. Example: (Before he went to the job interview), he got a haircut.

4) The COMPOUND-COMPLEX sentence contains TWO INDEPENDENT clauses joined by a conjunction or semicolon, and ONE OR MORE DEPENDENT clauses.

Example: (Bob is a doctor), and (he is a man) (who cares about people).

FOLLOW THESE RULES TO CLASSIFY SENTENCES EASILY:
1 - If you find a **conjunction or a semicolon and a complete sentence on both sides** of it, the sentence is **COMPOUND.**
2 - If you find an **adjective, adverb, or noun clause**, the sentence is **COMPLEX.**
3 - If you find **both 1 and 2 above**, the sentence is **COMPOUND/COMPLEX.**
4 - If you find **neither 1 nor 2 above**, the sentence is **SIMPLE.**

Example A
Hint: It will probably help to circle any conjunctions you find and to identify the dependent clauses, the ones that cannot stand alone as sentences, by placing them in parentheses.

Trees (that lose their leaves in winter) can usually withstand cold temperatures.

Explanation: There is no conjunction or semicolon, so the sentence cannot be compound.
(That lose their leaves in winter) is an adjective clause.
Classification: complex.

Example B

The manager of the restaurant **and** the owner of the pool hall are friends.
Explanation: There is a conjunction, but it joins two subjects, not two sentences. If you cover the word "and", you will see that "the manager of the restaurant" is not a complete sentence. This sentence is not a compound sentence.
There is no subordinate clause (adjective, adverb, or noun clause in this sentence.) This sentence is not complex.
Classification: simple

Example C

The teachers (who give clear directions) will usually get accurate responses from their students, **and** their students will get better grades.

Explanation:
The conjunction "and" joins two complete sentences.
(who give clear directions) is an adjective clause.
Classification: compound/complex

You can do it now!

Now that you have completed all 8 of the Simple Steps to Sentence Analysis, you should be able to take a sentence from any book and analyze it. You should also be able to write sentences of your own that are just as effective as those you find in literature.

Here are two sentences from my novel, *The Cowboy's Treasure*.

Analyze each of them (go through all 8 steps), and then write a sentence of your own. Be sure that all the words in your sentence are different, but the pattern remains the same.

Sentence 1
If he didn't make it back by the first of the year with the money, Sara would lose the home place and the whole trip would have been for nothing.

Sentence 2
He dug in the pocket of his damp jacket and removed a small package wrapped in crumpled newspaper.

I hope this book has been helpful. I know that if you follow the 8 simple steps, you will be successful.

Made in the USA
Las Vegas, NV
20 May 2024

90142565R00017